Firefighter Mindset
'How to overcome anything'

Kevin Thomas Quinn

Copyright © 2025 Kevin Quinn

All rights reserved, including the right to reproduce this book, or portions thereof in any form. No part of this text may be reproduced, transmitted, downloaded, decompiled, reverse engineered, or stored in any form or introduced into any information storage and retrieval system, in any form or by any means, whether electronic or mechanical without the express written permission of the author.

The views expressed in this work are solely those of the author and do not necessarily reflect the views of the publisher, and the publisher hereby disclaims any responsibility for them.

ISBN: 978-1-918038-50-7

This book was written primarily for my son, Kieran, who I love dearly; in case Daddy may not always be by his side to guide him, hopefully these words will.

Contents

Introduction - How To Overcome Anything 1

Chapter One - The Firefighter Mindset 5

Chapter Two - Make the Decision 13

Chapter Three - The S.E.A. of Change 23

Chapter Four - The 6 A's to Succeed 31

Chapter Five - Assess 41

Chapter Six - Accept 49

Chapter Seven - Adapt 57

Chapter Eight - Act 65

Chapter Nine - Accomplish 73

Chapter Ten - Appreciate 81

Chapter Eleven - Firefighter Fitness 89

Chapter Twelve - The Conclusion 97

Introduction

How To Overcome Anything

This book was written with one simple intention: to help anyone facing adversity or seeking to overcome challenges in life or work. Whether you're struggling with a personal setback, striving toward a dream, or navigating the unpredictable waves of daily life, this book offers a structured, practical system for moving forward with strength and clarity.

Now, imagine being unstoppable—able to face any obstacle with confidence, knowing you have the tools to overcome it. The Firefighter Mindset equips you with a reliable, adaptable process that can be applied to any hardship, goal, or dream. This is not theory—it's a proven system inspired by real professionals who confront danger, uncertainty, and pressure every single day.

This book is a guide—a blueprint—for consistently overcoming challenges and achieving success. It's about sustaining your wins, building resilience, and creating lasting, positive change in your life.

Trust, Discernment, and Personal Power

Trust should never be given lightly. Trust people only when their actions consistently reflect integrity—not their words, but their behaviour over time. Keep your circle small and filled with honourable individuals. Be cautious, not paranoid. Be wise, not cynical.

There are no "experts" who know it all—just people with experience. A bully is merely a coward in disguise. And you? You are not a coward. You are not lost. You have within you the power to grow, to act, to succeed.

Listen to yourself. Follow your own path. Stay away from toxic, negative people. Surround yourself with those who uplift you and share your values. Your worth is not defined by others. You are enough—just as you are.

On Confidence, Substance, and Strength

Avoid substances that cloud your judgment or offer false confidence. You don't need drugs or alcohol to feel secure or brave. True confidence comes from within—from knowing who you are, embracing your worth, and taking control of your life.

Live with intention. Be yourself, unapologetically. Seek out great days, love, and peace. Never seek conflict, but always be ready to stand your ground if needed. A warrior doesn't start a fight—but finishes it if they must.

The Power of Kindness

Kindness is not weakness—it's strength. It can disarm, confuse, and even protect you from enemies who underestimate it. Yet it is also a pure and powerful expression of love when given to those who deserve it. Use kindness wisely: as both shield and gift.

Be kind to all, not because everyone is worthy, but because it shapes you into someone worthy of peace and purpose.

Purpose, Gratitude, and Karma

Purpose gives life direction. Without it, you're like a ship lost at sea or a plane without a destination. Find something you're passionate about—something that fuels your spirit and moves you forward. Purpose brings happiness, strength, and mental clarity.

Be grateful for both the good times and the tough ones. Gratitude aligns you with positive energy and opens the door to good karma. Believe in cause and effect. Good or bad, what you put into the world comes back to you—maybe not as judgment, but as consequence.

Do good deliberately. Act with integrity. Keep your soul clean. Live in truth, and love will follow.

Final Thought: Judgement and Perception

It's okay to judge a book by its cover—just be willing to read it before you decide what it's truly about. First impressions matter, but deeper understanding always reveals the truth.

Chapter One

The Firefighter Mindset

Harnessing Your Inner Fire

Anger can be a powerful motivator when used constructively. It can fuel ambition, ignite change, and drive us to achieve great things. But hatred and bitterness? They corrode from within. Holding on to resentment is like drinking poison and expecting someone else to suffer. It only harms you.

Jealousy and envy are not signs that others are ahead—they are signs that you are not moving. If you're envious, it's time to wake up and take action. Start building your life. Your future begins the moment you decide to take ownership of it.

And always remember this: true love has no conditions.

What Is the Firefighter Mindset?

The Firefighter Mindset is a strategy—a way of thinking, acting, and living that I developed over 30 years of service in the London Fire Brigade. It's the product of real-world experience, forged through countless challenges, life-threatening situations, and moments of deep personal adversity.

As a firefighter and officer, I faced immense pressure. Fires don't wait. Lives are at stake. There's no room for hesitation. You must respond with clarity, courage, and control. Over time, I built a personal system—a mental and physical toolbox—for not only surviving these situations but thriving through them. I call it the Firefighter Mindset.

It is not an official procedure of the fire brigade. It is my own philosophy. My way of thinking. My code. And now, it's a system I share with you, in the hope it will help you face your own battles—whether in work, health, relationships, or life itself.

Tested in Fire—Forged in Life

This mindset didn't only serve me on duty—it saved me in my personal life.

I've faced divorce, trauma, depression, and even suicidal thoughts. I've been physically broken and mentally exhausted. After a catastrophic workplace accident in 2017—an explosion that caused severe and incurable acoustic shock—I lost sleep, clarity, and my sense of self.

The ringing in my ears was relentless. It kept me awake at night, robbed me of peace, and pushed me into the darkest mental space I'd ever known. Depression and anxiety took hold. I gained five stone. I was out of shape, out of breath, and out of hope.

And then came the moment of truth.

On December 18, 2018, I stood at the edge of London Bridge, staring down into the River Thames, seriously contemplating ending my life. I was broken. Tired. Ready to surrender.

But then, I thought of my two-year-old son. His smile. His love. His need for a father.

In that moment, I found my why. My reason to live. My reason to fight.

And so, I stepped back from the edge.

Find Your WHY

If you're in the darkest chapter of your life, the first step isn't just to act—it's to feel. Feel the reason that matters more than your pain. That's your why. Your anchor. Your fuel.

When you find your why, the rest is process: consistent action, determination, and never giving up.

'The Firefighter Mindset begins here: find your why, then fight on.'

From Surviving to Thriving

I used my own system to lose five stone in nine months and earn a spot in the 2023 national firefighter calendar. But more than that, I reclaimed my health, self-worth, and purpose.

This book is not written by a guru or expert. I'm not here to preach. I'm just a man who's been through the flames—literally and figuratively—and who came out stronger on the other side. If this mindset worked for me, it can work for you.

Even if this book helps just one person, it will have been worth it.

Why the Firefighter Mindset Works

When a firefighter arrives at a scene, there's no room for guesswork. Lives depend on immediate, effective action. Every second counts. This mindset must be focused, decisive, and relentless.

Now imagine applying that same system to your own life—when facing debt, heartbreak, illness, or loss. If you treat your challenges with the same urgency, clarity, and discipline, you'll see real results. The Firefighter Mindset is failproof because it's forged in situations where failure simply isn't an option.

Faith: The Unseen Force

There's one more thing the Firefighter Mindset requires—faith.

Whether you believe in God, the universe, or simply in yourself, you must believe. Faith is the ability to see the outcome before it manifests. It's the invisible force that powers your actions, fuels your courage, and silences doubt.

Faith means trusting that your journey has a purpose, even when it's painful. That you are not alone. That you are capable, and worthy, and enough.

Call it God, fate, your inner warrior, or your soul—it doesn't matter. What matters is that you believe.

Final Thoughts

The Firefighter Mindset is not just an attitude—it's a system backed by action. It has helped me survive trauma, recover from injury, rebuild my life, and rediscover my purpose.

Now, it's your turn.

If you're facing adversity, loss, or a dream that feels out of reach—remember this:

1. Find your WHY.
2. Believe you can overcome.
3. Take consistent action.
4. Never give up.
5. Have faith.

You are not alone. You are stronger than you know.

You have the power within you to rise, rebuild, and win.

So, keep going.

Be courageous. Be kind. Be relentless.

Live with the Firefighter Mindset.

Real-World Application: From Fireground to Life

Chapter 1 – The Firefighter Mindset

On the fireground, having the right mindset is everything. It means being mentally prepared to face danger, making clear decisions under pressure, and staying calm amid chaos. This mindset is developed through training, experience, and discipline. It keeps firefighters focused on their mission and their team's safety.

In life, adopting the Firefighter Mindset means cultivating mental toughness, resilience, and a proactive attitude. Challenges and setbacks are inevitable, but with the right mindset, you approach them with confidence and purpose. This mindset helps you stay committed to your goals, handle stress effectively, and lead yourself through difficult times—just like you would on the fireground.

Chapter 1: Introduction to the Firefighter Mindset

Worksheet: Define Your Mindset

1. What does the term Firefighter Mindset mean to you?

2. Reflect on a time when you faced extreme pressure. How did you respond?

3. What core values guide your actions in adversity?

4. What would "no option but win" look like in your own life?

5. Who or what are you responsible for when it matters most?

Journal Prompt

"In a crisis, I respond with…"

Describe your automatic responses in high-stress situations. How do you want to evolve those responses using the Firefighter Mindset?

Chapter Two

Make the Decision

My Background – A Firefighter's Calling

I was born in Lewisham Hospital in 1970 and raised in Eltham, southeast London. From as early as I can remember, I was obsessed with becoming a firefighter. Every time I saw a fire engine roar past, lights flashing and sirens blaring, my heart would race. I knew they were going to help someone, and I wanted to be one of them.

At 14, I wrote a letter to the London Fire Brigade, asking to join. They replied kindly—but firmly: "Come back when you're 18." I did exactly that. At 18, I applied, but didn't get through the initial stage. Disappointed but undeterred, I waited for the next recruitment round and reapplied at 20. This time, I passed every part of the process. But due to a backlog of new recruits, I had to wait another two years before I could begin training.

Finally, on Monday, 24 May 1993, I walked into the Southwark Training Centre near London Bridge. I was 22 years old—young, nervous, and slightly naive—but determined. It was the beginning of a life-changing journey.

Why I Chose This Life

In hindsight, my passion for firefighting wasn't just about the job—it was about what firefighters symbolised. To me, they represented reliability, strength, and unwavering commitment. They were people who showed up in your worst moments and didn't leave until you were safe.

When I was just seven, my father left our family. My mum, my older brother, and I were left to figure life out alone. Deep down, I think firefighting represented the dependable, honourable father figure I didn't have. Firefighters, in my eyes, were the embodiment of loyalty and courage—men and women who never quit on anyone.

That belief has never left me. Even today, I still see firefighters as the ultimate example of strength, fortitude, and purpose.

Never Give Up, Never Leave Anyone Behind

A firefighter doesn't quit. We show up in the most desperate moments. We walk into burning buildings when everyone else is running out. We deal with the chaos. We fight through the fear. We don't leave until the job is done.

That mentality became my code.

It might sound dramatic or even "cheesy" in today's world, but I believe in it wholeheartedly:

No one is forgotten. Everyone is saveable.

We go—you go. Never surrender. Never give up. There is always hope.

The Ultimate Choice: Quit or Fight

Over the years—both in my fire service career and in my personal life—I've come to realise something powerful:

There is one decision that will shape every challenge you face: Will you quit, or will you fight?

This decision defines your outcomes. It is the first and most important choice you make when adversity strikes. Everything else flows from it.

At a fire scene, firefighters don't weigh up whether they feel like pushing forward. We've already made the decision long before the incident ever occurred. We don't quit. We fight. Always.

That's what separates the Firefighter Mindset from other approaches to life:

The decision to fight is made before the pressure comes.

Imagine applying that mindset to your own life. You'd be unstoppable.

My Personal Inferno

Life doesn't just test you at work—it tests you at home, in the heart, in the soul.

I was married for eight years when I came home one day to an empty house. My wife had left, taking our four-year-old son and half the furniture. I was devastated, broken in every way. But I knew I had to decide:

Do I quit, or do I fight?

I chose to fight—for my son, for his safety, for my future.

It wasn't easy. I was out of shape and overwhelmed. But I applied the Firefighter Mindset to my personal crisis. I didn't give up. I fought relentlessly.

Today, my son is safe. I have a strong co-parenting relationship with his mother. And that only happened because I made the decision not to quit.

From Broken to Rebuilt

At my lowest, I was overweight, depressed, and unrecognisable from the man I once was. But I clawed my way back.

In fact, over three decades I appeared in the official Firefighter Calendar three times—at ages 28, 38, and 51. In between, I even did glamour modelling for The Sun and other national newspapers.

That might sound surprising, but it proves one thing: with the right mindset and consistent action, you can always come back stronger—physically, mentally, and emotionally.

Face the Fire or Drown in It

Here's a simple truth I've learned:

You either face the problem—or you drown in it.

Avoiding a problem is no different than giving in to it. Whether it's health, money, relationships, or trauma—if you do nothing, the situation will consume you.

For example:

- If you're in debt, go to the bank. Set up a payment plan. Take control.
- If you ignore it, the problem grows. Interest piles up. Anxiety increases. Maybe you even spiral downwards and drink to cope, shut people out, avoid the truth.

The outcome is the same: you drown—just more slowly.

But if you choose to face the fire, even if it's scary, messy, or overwhelming, you give yourself a chance to win.

The Firefighter Mindset in Everyday Life

This book isn't about heroics. It's about survival—and thriving.

The Firefighter Mindset is a system of thought and action designed to help you:

- Tackle adversity head-on
- Stay physically and mentally resilient
- Maintain clarity under pressure
- Turn trauma into triumph

Built from 30 years of frontline firefighting and personal battles, this mindset saved my life. Now it's here to help you reclaim yours.

You Must Change to Win

If you want to achieve your goals, you must change. You can't overcome life's trials by staying the same. You must evolve. You must act.

Whether you're broken, betrayed, broke, or battling something in silence—you still have a choice.

Will you give up?

Or will you fight?

🔥 Real-World Application: From Fireground to Life

Chapter 2 – Make the Decision

In the fire service, hesitation can be deadly. When the tones drop and the call comes in, firefighters don't sit around debating whether they feel like going. The decision to act was made long before the fire. You committed the day you joined the watch, trained for the job, and showed up for shift change. When you're inside a smoke-logged building, crawling low to rescue a trapped civilian, there's no time for second-guessing. Every move, every breath, every decision matters. Decisiveness keeps people alive.

In life, the same principle applies. You can't wait until everything feels perfect or the stars align. Whether it's ending a toxic relationship, starting a new business, or getting healthy—you must make the decision. Not just casually, but fully. No more dipping a toe in the water. Decide, then burn the boats. No backup plan. No excuses. That's the mindset of a firefighter—and of anyone who's serious about change.

It's not just about taking action. It's about becoming someone who's already decided—someone who's committed, even when it's hard. That's the moment everything changes.

Fireground Lesson ➜ Life Lesson:

Just like on a call, hesitation costs time, and time can cost lives. In your personal life, hesitation costs dreams—and your future self might pay the price. Decide now, before the flames surround you.

Workshop Chapter 2 – Make the Decision

To move from indecision to full commitment by crafting a clear, actionable personal decision—just like committing to a call without hesitation.

Identify the Decision

What is one major decision in your life you've been avoiding, delaying, or approaching half-heartedly?

Example: "I need to decide whether to stay in a job that drains me every day or finally pursue the thing I am passionate about."

Write Your Why:

Why is making this decision important? What's at stake if you don't decide?

Example: "If I don't change, I'll stay burnt out and miss the chance to live with purpose."

Seal It with a Signature:

Sign a personal commitment contract below to reflect the full decision—no turning back.

Personal Commitment Contract

I, _____, hereby make the clear and final decision to:

I understand that indecision is a decision in itself—and it will not serve me.

Signed: _____

Date: _____

Take the First Action:

Right now, list one step you can take in the next 24 hours to reinforce your decision.

Example: "Make that call you need to make to begin the journey towards you real purpose in life."

Reflect on how hesitation has held you back and describe how your mindset would shift if you approached that decision like a firefighter approaches a call: trained, committed, and all-in.

Journal Prompt:

"What decision have I delayed out of fear, comfort, or uncertainty—and how would my life change if I committed to it fully today?"

Chapter Three

The S.E.A. of Change

The S.E.A. of Change is a system I developed to help people understand the stages required to make real, lasting change in their lives. Whether you're stuck in an unhappy situation, facing hardship, or striving toward a dream you've never achieved before—you must change. And to change your situation, more often than not, you'll first need to change yourself.

To do something you've never done before, you must think in a way you've never thought before. If you do the same as everyone else, you be the same as everyone else. That's why understanding how change works is vital. This chapter walks you through that transformation using the S.E.A. of Change—Start, Endure, Accomplish.

It may sound simple, but simplicity often holds the greatest truth. These three steps are not just theoretical—they're practical stages that you will experience during any meaningful change. When you know what's coming, you're better prepared to handle it and succeed.

Start – The Courage to Begin

Every transformation begins with a decision—the decision to fight, to move forward to no longer stay where you are. It takes faith, self-belief, and courage to take that first step. Without the decision to start, nothing else matters.

Some people never begin. They give up before even trying. They surrender to their circumstances, convinced that nothing can change. That's not going to be you.

You've picked up this book. That alone tells me something important—you already have the spark. You already believe that change is possible. Now it's time to act. You don't need to have all the answers. You just need to start.

Even if you're unsure, start anyway. The path will reveal itself as you go. Thinking about change isn't enough. You must act.

Ask yourself:

- What am I fighting for?
- Why do I want this?
- Who am I doing this for?

That's your WHY—your What Helps You. Your WHY is the fire that keeps you going through the storm.

You also need a vision—a clear picture of what success looks like. What does your life look like after the change? Who are you on the other side of it?

To help define that, I use The Three W's:

- What has happened?
- Why do I need to change it?
- Where do I want to be?

Answer these honestly. Not emotionally, but practically. Emotions can cloud your judgment. You need to see clearly.

If you're going through a divorce, for example, assess how best to protect yourself and your children—financially, emotionally, and physically. Set your emotions aside and make a practical plan.

Practical doesn't mean boring or small. If your dream feels impossible to others, ignore those people. If your WHY is strong enough and your plan solid, you can do anything. There are no rules to what you can achieve. If you WHY is big enough you can overcome any how.

Endure – The Strength to Keep Going

Endurance is where most people give up. It's the hard part. It tests you. This is the part where you'll be challenged the most.

But let me tell you this: the pain is temporary. The strength you gain from pushing through will last forever. You will be a new person that can endure anything.

To endure, you need patience, discipline, and perseverance. You will have days when progress feels invisible. Keep going. You will have setbacks. Keep going.

This stage might last weeks, months, or even years. But you will come through it stronger, wiser, and proud of yourself.

If you quit, regret will follow. You'll always wonder: What if I'd kept going? Don't leave space for that question. Endure.

Celebrate the small wins. They matter. During dark times, even something like paying a bill, going to the gym, or getting a haircut can be a victory. Don't underestimate what you achieve, just by showing up for yourself is a win.

Every small positive action—exercise, eating well, staying focused—adds up to long-term success. Likewise, negative habits like smoking, taking drugs and excessive drinking, or even constant complaining will pull you down. Choose wisely.

Even when it's tough, stay on the thin path—a narrow road of focus, discipline, and self-control. It may feel boring at times, but it leads to an exciting, successful future.

And above all—be grateful. A grateful heart cannot coexist with bitterness or depression. Start each day with gratitude, even if it's for the smallest things. Gratitude builds optimism, and optimism builds resilience.

Accomplish – The Power to Finish

Accomplishment is the final and most satisfying part of the S.E.A. of Change. You've started. You've endured. Now you must finish.

Your change—your goal, your dream—is waiting for you at the end. All the effort, pain, and struggle lead to this moment. You are not the same person you were when you started. You've grown. You've developed. You've transformed.

It doesn't matter how long it takes. What matters is that you complete the journey. Be relentless in your belief that you will get there. You must be resolute in your mind, body, and soul—this is your mission.

Remember: Success is not luck. It's the outcome of repeated action, belief, and endurance.

Let me share a few final principles to carry with you:

- Be humble. Keep your victories to yourself just as you would your failures.
- Give back. Support others. Consider giving to charity and investing in your future.

- Stay focused. Avoid distractions like excessive drinking, drugs, or toxic people.
- Forgive failure. In yourself and others. It's how we grow.
- Be kind—even to enemies. But never let your guard down again. Be gracious in victory, but always aware.

And when it matters—when your life, your family, your future is on the line—you must win. There is no option to lose. Get the job done. That's the Firefighter Mindset.

You have everything you need inside you to fight, overcome, and win. Never forget that.

Start. Endure. Accomplish. Ride the S.E.A. of Change.

Real-World Application: From Fireground to Life

Chapter 3 – Change

On the fireground, change is constant and often unpredictable—whether it's shifting weather, evolving fire behaviour, or sudden emergencies. Firefighters must stay flexible, adapt tactics, and think quickly. Resistance to change can cost lives, while embracing it can mean the difference between success and disaster.

In life, change is just as inevitable. Learning to accept and work with change, rather than fight it, builds resilience. Whether it's a new job, relationship, or challenge, the ability to pivot and grow with change helps you overcome setbacks and seize new opportunities. Embrace change like you would on the fireground: stay alert, stay prepared, and keep moving forward.

Workshop Chapter 2: The S.E.A. of Change

(Stop. Examine. Adjust.)

Worksheet: SEA Your Situation

1. STOP: What situation in your life needs you to pause right now?

2. EXAMINE: What facts, emotions, and consequences do you see in this situation?

3. ADJUST: What changes can you realistically make to shift this situation positively?

Bonus: Identify where you usually rush or avoid one of the SEA steps.

Journal Prompt

"When I take a step back and examine my life, I notice..."

Reflect on patterns, blind spots, or unhelpful reactions that show up when change is needed.

Chapter Four

The 6 A's to Succeed

Success, in any walk of life—whether on the fireground, in business, or in your personal journey—relies on mindset. The Firefighter Mindset is built on two powerful frameworks: the S.E.A. of Change (explored in the previous chapter) and The 6 A's to Succeed—a proven method I developed through 30 years of front-line service in the London Fire Brigade.

This is not an official doctrine of the fire brigade—it is my personal system, forged through real-life experience. From battling fires to leading crews through complex rescues, I used this process to consistently overcome adversity and deliver outcomes when failure was not an option.

Introducing the 6 A's

The 6 A's to Succeed is a structured, repeatable approach for tackling problems, achieving goals, and sustaining progress. The six steps are:

1. Assess
2. Accept
3. Adapt
4. Act
5. Accomplish
6. Appreciate

These steps can be applied to virtually any challenge: from mental health struggles and personal hardships to business ventures and fitness goals. They represent a progression—from understanding the problem, to taking decisive action, and finally, to sustaining success and recognising your growth.

Why This System Works

The fireground teaches you that there's no room for hesitation, excuses, or failure. Firefighters are the last line of defence. No one else is coming. You either succeed—or lives are lost. That reality sharpens your mindset and forces a total commitment to outcome.

The Firefighter Mindset embodies:

- Resilience – You must endure.
- Responsibility – You must take ownership.
- Resourcefulness – You must find a way to win.

Every emergency incident demands quick thinking, adaptability, and resolve—just like the challenges you face in life or business. That's why the 6 A's work. They follow a natural order of human response in crisis, but make it conscious, deliberate, and repeatable.

Using the 6 A's in Your Life

Let's walk through each step briefly, before diving deeper in the following chapters:

1. Assess

You must fully understand your situation—what happened, what it means, and what it demands. Use the Three W's:

- What happened?
- Why must I act?
- Where do I want to be?

This step switches on your awareness and puts you in control. You can't solve what you don't see.

2. Accept

Facing uncomfortable truths is the next step. You must accept your current reality, your role in it, and your responsibility to change it. Denial delays growth. Acceptance opens the door.

3. Adapt

Now, create your plan. It must be:

- Methodical
- Ambitious
- Punctual

I call this a MAP Plan. Set clear targets. Timeframe your goals. Don't be afraid to dream big—be bold. Whether it's losing weight, starting a business, or rebuilding after a setback, detail how you'll do it.

4. Act

Ideas mean nothing without execution. Decide to act. Commit fully. Find your "Why"—your reason for pushing through the hard times. Without action, you stay stuck.

5. Accomplish

When you act on your plan, you will progress. Success might not come all at once—but stay consistent, and results will follow. If you fall off, regroup and go again. Winning becomes a habit.

6. Appreciate

Celebrate your progress. Gratitude reinforces growth. By appreciating how far you've come, you build confidence that you can do it again. You also develop the emotional resilience to face the next challenge.

Real-World Application: From Fireground to Life

The 6 A's to Succeed

On the fireground, success doesn't happen by accident — it's the result of clear action under pressure. Every successful incident follows the 6 A's, whether we know it or not. You Assess the scene — size it up fast. You Accept the conditions — you don't whine about the smoke, you adapt. You take Action — decisive, effective movement that makes progress. You Adjust as new threats emerge — fire spreads, structures collapse, priorities change. You Advance — room to room, inch by inch, until the job is done. And then you Achieve — not just by putting the fire out, but by saving lives, preserving property, and returning home better than you arrived.

In life, the same framework applies. Want to change careers, start a business, improve your health, fix a broken relationship? Run it through the 6 A's. Assess where you're really at. Accept the brutal truth, no excuses. Take bold action. Adjust when the plan meets resistance. Advance, even if slowly. And in time, you'll achieve something meaningful.

Every fire has unknowns. So does life. The difference is whether you charge forward with a plan — or stand back and watch it all burn.

Firefighter Mindset and Mental Health

No discussion of success is complete without talking about mental health—a topic often overlooked, especially by those in high-pressure roles.

The 6 A's Applied to Mental Health

Assess

Notice when something feels off—anger, sadness, guilt, apathy. Are your behaviours changing? Are you withdrawing or obsessing? Self-awareness is the first win.

Accept

It's okay to not be okay. Accept where you are without shame. Denial keeps you stuck. Acceptance starts your healing.

Adapt

Create a MAP Plan:

- Methodical – Track patterns, seek support, build structure.
- Ambitious – Set a bold intention to heal and thrive.
- Punctual – Use timeframes and goals to stay focused.

Visualise a future where you feel strong again—no matter how dark it seems now.

Act

Do something. Get help. Exercise. Talk to someone. Don't wait for motivation. Start with discipline. Find your

WHY—maybe your kids, your dreams, or even proving to yourself that you still matter.

Accomplish

Progress is the win, not perfection. You may have setbacks—but the act of getting up again is a sign of success.

Appreciate

Take pride in the fact that you've fought back. You did the work. You are resilient. You are capable. And you can repeat this system again whenever needed.

Final Thoughts on the 6 A's to succeed

Every time I responded to a fire, I had no guarantees. But what I did have was a system—a way to take control and push through. That system became the 6 A's to succeed.

It's helped me lead fire crews, build my life, recover from personal losses, and achieve goals I once thought impossible. And now, I'm sharing it with you—not because I read it in a book, but because I lived it.

You don't need to be a firefighter to adopt this mindset. You just need to commit. You need to believe that you are the answer to your own challenges.

There are no shortcuts, and no one else is coming to help you.

It is down to you to help yourself, always remember that.

But the good news? You're enough. And with the 6 A's, you now have a map to guide you through to win.

❄ Workshop Chapter 4. The 6 A's to Succeed – Overview

(Assess, Accept, Adapt, Act, Accomplish, Appreciate)

Worksheet: Snapshot of the 6 A's

1. Choose one goal or problem you are facing.

2. Write a one-line summary of what each of the 6 A's would mean for that situation.

    Assess:

    Accept:

    Adapt:

    Act:

    Accomplish:

    Appreciate:

3. Which step do you usually skip or struggle with? Why?

Use the 3W Framework:

1. What happened?
2. Why must I do something about it?
3. Where do I want to be?

Bonus Questions:

- What areas of your life (physical, emotional, financial, spiritual) need the most attention right now?
- What practical first steps would move you forward?

Journal Prompt

"The part of change I avoid most is..."

Explore what makes certain parts of transformation harder for you and what's at the root of that.

"If I were being 100% honest about my current situation, I'd admit that..."

Get real with yourself—write as if no one else will ever read this. Pure honesty is the first courageous step.

Chapter Five

Assess

Step 1 of the 6 A's to Succeed

If you want to change your life—whether it's to overcome adversity, solve a difficult problem, or chase a dream—you must begin with one thing:

Assessment

Change doesn't happen by accident. Transformation starts with awareness. To accomplish anything meaningful in life, you'll go through three stages:

1. Start
2. Endure
3. Accomplish

But to start, you must assess where you are—mentally, physically, emotionally, spiritually, and financially. This is the foundational step in the 6 A's to Succeed. Without a clear understanding of your present situation, you won't know how far you have to go—or even what direction to move in.

Be Brutally Honest with Yourself

This is not about your past or your dreams of the future—this is about right now.

Where are you, truthfully?

This is where you must strip away the noise. No excuses. No lies to yourself. No sugar-coating. You must look at your situation through a clear lens—without emotion, without judgment—just truth.

For example:

- If you're going through a separation, assess how you'll protect yourself and your children—legally, financially, emotionally.
- If you're trying to get fit, assess your current health, habits, and limitations. What's your weight? Your fitness level? Your nutrition?
- If you're facing financial struggles, assess your income, expenses, debts, and obligations. Write it all down.

This is not the time to be sentimental. Emotions like anger, bitterness, jealousy, or shame will cloud your judgment. This is about strategic clarity—what needs to be done to survive and then thrive.

Practical Doesn't Mean Playing Small

When I say your assessment needs to be practical, I'm not telling you to limit your dreams.

I'm saying: dream big—but plan with detail.

Practical means laying out the steps that will bridge the gap between where you are and where you want to be.

For example:

- If you need a solicitor, figure out how to raise the money.

- If you want to lose weight, identify the food you'll eat, the exercise you'll do, and the time frame you're giving yourself.
- If your dream is to be in the Firefighter Calendar (yes, I've been there!), that dream starts with a practical plan: meals, workouts, deadlines, and discipline.

This is how big dreams become real goals.

Your Will Determines Your Reality

Never let others tell you what's possible. People will say:

- "That's not realistic."
- "That's too ambitious."
- "You're not being practical."

Ignore them.

You're not here to live their version of reality. If your will is strong enough, if your "why" is powerful enough, you can achieve what others call impossible. There are no rules to what you can or cannot do—except the ones you accept as true.

Life Is a Train Journey – Don't Miss the View

Life is a constant rhythm of calm and chaos, peace and problems. But here's the truth: adversity will come and go—just like the good times.

Don't ruin your peaceful moments by obsessing over past pain or fearing the future. When you're in a good season, recognise it. Appreciate it. Don't cloud it with regret or anxiety.

Think of life like a train journey. You know the destination—we all do. It's the journey that counts. Along the way, the train will stop at different stations—some good, some bad. You'll meet fellow passengers—some kind, some not. But through it all, the view is there if you choose to look out the window.

Some people sleep through life. Some worry every mile. But some—the wise ones—choose to look out the window and marvel at the view. They choose to live. They choose to experience.

Be that person.

Closing Thoughts: The Power of Step One

The assessment stage is not about judgment. It's not about guilt. It's about clarity.

This step gives you the foundation to move forward with confidence, not confusion.

So pause, breathe, and take a real look at where you are right now.

Write it down.

Own it.

Only then can you build your plan and move into the next phase of the 6 A's—Acceptance.

You can do this.

Next up: Accept – Step 2 of the 6 A's to Succeed

Real-World Application: From Fireground to Life

Chapter 5 – Assess

Before you commit to a door, a ladder, or a tactic on the fireground, you assess. You size up the smoke, the structure, the hazards. You read the room — literally. Because one bad call in your assessment can cost someone their life.

Life is no different. Most people rush in emotionally, react impulsively, or blindly follow what everyone else is doing. But the firefighter mindset teaches you to pause and evaluate — your situation, your resources, your risks. Whether it's your career, a relationship, or a financial decision, if you don't assess the truth of where you are and what's in front of you, you're setting yourself up for a burn you won't recover from.

Good assessment isn't about overthinking. It's about being clear-eyed and honest. In the fire service, a bad size-up can kill your team. In life, a bad one can waste years, ruin relationships, or destroy your future.

Train yourself to assess with courage — not with fear. Then act with clarity. That's how you stay alive and move forward on the fireground and in life.

Here's a worksheet and journal prompt designed to go with Chapter Five – Assess (Step 1 of the 6 A's to Succeed). These tools will help the reader practically apply what they've just learned and begin the transformation process.

🔧 Worksheet: ASSESS – Step 1 of the 6 A's to Succeed

✅ Section 1: Where Am I Right Now?

Be honest and objective. Rate each area of your life from 1 (struggling) to 10 (thriving) and add notes for each:

Area   Rating (1-10)   Notes – What's Going On?

Mental Health

Physical Health

Emotional State

Financial Position

Career/Work

Relationships

Spiritual Life

✅ Section 2: What Happened?

Briefly describe the current problem, challenge, or adversity you're facing.

- What happened?

✅ Section 3: Why Must I Do This?

Write down your reasons for change. Why does this matter to you? What's driving you to overcome this situation?

- Why must I do this?

✅ Section 4: Where Do I Want to Be?

Get specific. Think big but be clear.

- What does success look like in this situation?
- What would your life look like if this challenge was resolved?
- Where do I want to be?

✅ Section 5: What's the Practical Path?

Don't worry about making it perfect. This is about sketching the real-world steps you'll need to take.

Examples:
- Contact solicitor
- Set budget
- Plan exercise and meal routine
- Apply for job or course
- My first practical actions are:

📓 **Journal Prompt:** The Power of the Present Moment

"To change my life, I must first understand my life as it is right now."

Take 10–15 minutes to write freely in response to this prompt:

✍️ "What is my current reality—and what am I pretending not to see?"

Explore the parts of your life that are out of alignment. Don't filter it. Let your truth come out without judgment. This is just between you and the page. The more honest you are, the more powerful your transformation will be.

Chapter Six

Accept

Step 2 of the 6 A's to Succeed

"Acceptance is not surrender. It is the first step toward taking control."

Face the Truth

There's no cavalry coming. No one else is going to rescue you from your current situation. As harsh as that may sound, it's liberating—because the power to change your life lies within you. The moment you accept that truth is the moment you begin to reclaim control.

To accept is not to approve of what's happened, but to acknowledge it fully. Whatever you're going through—loss, heartbreak, betrayal, failure—has already happened. Your job now is not to change the past but to change the outcome that follows.

Accepting reality puts you in a position to do something about it.

Take Responsibility

When you take ownership, you take power. That doesn't mean blaming yourself for things beyond your control—it means recognizing your power to respond. Your choices, actions, and mindset from this moment forward are within your grasp.

Victim or victor: the choice is yours. Doing nothing is still a decision. And if you choose that route, accept the consequences—don't become bitter. But if you want victory, it begins here.

You must stand in the mirror and say:

"This is my life. I will face it. I will change it."

Control Your Emotions – Don't Let Them Control You

Your emotions are like fire—controlled, they can warm and light your path. Uncontrolled, they can burn everything down.

Anger, grief, fear—these are natural. But don't make permanent decisions based on temporary feelings. Use your emotions for clarity, not confusion. Respond, don't react.

Stay cool. Stay sharp. Win smart.

Discipline Over Motivation

Motivation fades. Discipline remains.

Discipline is the muscle you build that carries you through the hard days. It's the repetition of action even when you don't feel like it. You must act like the person you want to become before you feel like that person.

Discipline turns dreams into results. Discipline fuels your journey from where you are to where you need to be.

Failure Isn't Final

You will fall. That's a promise. But every time you fall, you gather data. You reset, realign, and reengage.

Failure is a stepping stone—it redirects your path, not defines it. Keep going.

Faith. Will. Discipline.

These three will carry you:

- Faith to believe it's possible.
- Will to push forward despite fear.
- Discipline to execute your plan daily.

Together, they form the backbone of your transformation.

You Are Not Alone

Accepting your situation doesn't mean isolating yourself. Seek your community—friends, family, books, professionals. Use every available support system. You don't have to do it alone, but you do have to lead your journey.

In the End, Fear Is Useless

We all leave this world eventually. When you realize that, you understand that fear of judgment, rejection, or failure is meaningless. Live your life fully, with courage. There's nothing more dangerous to fear than regret.

Real-World Application: From Fireground to Life

Chapter 6 – Accept

On the fireground, acceptance is critical. Sometimes, despite your best efforts, conditions are beyond control—a sudden flashover, a collapsed ceiling, or a lost victim. Accepting these harsh realities doesn't mean giving up; it means acknowledging the situation clearly so you can focus your energy on what you can control: safety, teamwork, and the next best action.

In life, acceptance works the same way. You'll face setbacks, loss, and situations that aren't fair or ideal. Resisting reality wastes precious energy and creates unnecessary suffering. When you accept what is, you can stop fighting the past or uncontrollable factors and start making peace. That peace gives you the clarity and calm to find solutions and move forward.

Acceptance is the foundation for resilience—both in firefighting and in life. It's not weakness; it's the strength to see things honestly and respond with courage.

🪶 **Worksheet** – Accept (Step 2 of the 6 A's)

Part 1: Acknowledge Your Reality

- What challenge, adversity, or problem are you currently facing?
- What part of this situation do you need to accept to move forward?

Part 2: Take Ownership

- In what ways can you take responsibility, even if the situation isn't your fault?

Part 3: Emotional Awareness

- Which emotions are clouding your judgment right now (anger, fear, sadness, etc.)?
- How can you manage them more effectively?

Part 4: Build Your Support System

- Who or what can support you right now (people, resources, habits)?

Part 5: Design a Micro-Action Plan

What small, disciplined actions can you take this week to begin changing your reality?

📝 Journal Prompt – Accept

Write freely for 10–15 minutes:

"What do I need to accept right now in order to move forward? What would it mean to stop wishing things were different—and instead start building from exactly where I am?"

Chapter Seven

Adapt

Step 3 of the 6 A's to Succeed

To survive and succeed, you must adapt. This is where change becomes action.

Adapt means action. It means direction. It means structure.

You've already assessed where you are and accepted your reality. Now it's time to plan, adjust, and move forward deliberately and methodically.

Start with Your Vision

Write down what you want to happen — but write it in the present tense.

Write it as if it's already real:

"I am financially free."

"I am healthy and strong."

"I am peaceful and purposeful."

This mindset shift programs your brain to see success as inevitable. It fuels your attitude, shapes your decisions, and guides your behaviour.

Use the M.A.P. Plan

To adapt successfully, you must follow a solid plan — your MAP Plan:

- M – Methodical: Design a step-by-step, clear path toward your goal.
- A – Ambitious: Set goals that excite and challenge you.
- P – Punctual: Time matters. Commit to deadlines. Track your progress.

Without this structure, energy is wasted. A scattered plan is no plan. A good plan is the backbone of any comeback.

Control Your Inputs

To adapt, you must create the best environment for progress:

- Eliminate distractions: No drinking, drugs, toxic entertainment, or gossip.
- Minimize negative influences. Surround yourself with positive, forward-thinking people.
- Speak success: Talk about progress, not just problems. Focus on where you're going, not what you've lost.
- Take care of your mind and body: Eat well. Move. Rest. Pause.
- Take breaks: Walk, laugh, watch a movie — not to escape, but to reset and recharge.

Regular Evaluation

Schedule regular moments to stop and reflect:
- Where am I on the path?
- What's working?
- What needs adjusting?
- How far have I come?

This allows you to course-correct before you get too far off track.

Balance the Three Life Zones

To adapt with purpose, you must align and manage these areas:

1. Life Areas:
- Family – Relationships, responsibilities, home.
- Business – Work, finances, career.
- Spiritual – Beliefs, peace, connection with something greater.

2. Self-Components:
- Health – Physical and mental fitness.
- Wealth – Money, knowledge, experiences, love.
- Soul – Purpose, meaning, faith, and alignment with the Universe.

Adapt and You Will Advance

Adapting is not abandoning who you are — it's becoming who you must be to succeed. It's responding, not reacting.

It's planning, not panicking.

It's owning your direction.

🔥 Real-World Application: From Fireground to Life

Chapter 7 – Adapt

On the fireground, nothing ever goes exactly as planned. Conditions change by the second—smoke thickens, walls weaken, new hazards emerge. The team that sticks rigidly to a plan without adapting will get caught out. But the crew that adjusts on the fly, who listens, thinks fast, and changes tactics? They're the ones who come out safe and successful.

Life throws curveballs the same way. You might have a plan for your career, your health, or your relationships—but when unexpected challenges hit, you've got to adapt. Holding tight to old habits or rigid thinking only leads to frustration, failure, and burnout.

Adaptation isn't about giving up your goals. It's about flexibility in the face of reality. It's learning from what's working and what's not. It's switching gears when the route you took is blocked. Just like on the fireground, adapting means survival—and thriving.

Train your mind to be agile. When life's smoke changes, don't panic—adapt, adjust, and push forward smarter and stronger.

Worksheet: Build Your MAP Plan

Part 1 – Write Your Goal in Present Tense

What is your goal? Write it as if it's already done.

Example: "I am in control of my finances and living debt-free."

Part 2 – Create Your MAP Plan

Methodical – What is the step-by-step plan to reach your goal?

1.
2.
3.

Ambitious – What bold result are you aiming for?

Punctual – What deadlines are you committing to?

Short-term:

Long-term:

Part 3 – Environmental Check

- What do you need to eliminate to create a better environment?
- What routines or habits can support your focus?

Part 4 – Three Life Zones Review

Rate and reflect on each area from 1–10:

Area   Score   Notes (What's Strong/Needs Work)

Family

Business/Work

Spiritual

Health

Wealth

Soul

 Journal Prompt: The Art of Adapting

"Where in my life have, I been resisting change? What would happen if I fully adapted, accepted the challenge, and started walking toward the version of myself I want to become?"

Use this prompt to uncover your own blocks — and how adapting can unlock your next level.

Chapter Eight

Act

Step 4 of the 6 A's to Succeed

So far, you've followed a path most never fully commit to. You've assessed your current situation with clear eyes. You've accepted the full reality of your life—no more denial, no more illusions. You've adapted, designing a MAP Plan: Methodical, Ambitious, and Punctual. Now, the time has come to take the most critical and transformational step of all:

Act.

There are only two parts to life: thinking and doing.

Thinking got you this far—it clarified your goals, exposed your truths, and built your plan. But thinking alone won't move mountains. It's time to shift gears. The only way forward now is action.

Don't wait for the perfect moment. Don't wait until you "feel ready." The truth is, you won't always feel ready. The secret is to act anyway. The power is in the doing.

Acting on Your MAP Plan

Your plan is the route. It's your lifeline from where you are now, to where you want to be. Just as a firefighter follows a clear, practiced protocol in the chaos of a blaze, you must follow your plan with discipline and determination.

You don't have to know every step in advance—you only need to take the next one. And then the next. Each action builds momentum, confidence, and results.

When the world seems unclear, go back to your MAP Plan:

- Methodical – Am I following the steps?
- Ambitious – Am I aiming high enough to transform?
- Punctual – Am I sticking to my deadlines?

Don't Think, Just Do

That phrase may sound reckless at first—but here's the deeper truth:

Overthinking is fear in disguise. It's hesitation dressed up as logic. It's your mind trying to protect you from imagined pain. But inaction creates far more regret than imperfect action ever could.

Acting doesn't mean being reckless—it means being committed.

So now, execute. Let your actions speak.

- Wake up early.
- Make that call.
- Submit that application.

- Start the workout.
- Show up, even if you're scared.

Ignore the Critics

When you begin to act boldly, others will notice. Some will cheer you on. Others may question, mock, or try to pull you back down.

That's not about you—it's about their own fears. You must stay grounded in your why, your plan, and your belief in yourself.

You don't owe anyone an explanation. This journey is yours.

Consistency Over Perfection

You won't be perfect every day. Some days you'll fall short. That's okay. The goal is not perfection—it's consistency.

Show up. Keep going. Even when it's hard. Especially when it's hard.

Because every action, no matter how small, compounds over time. Just like drops of water carve through rock, your daily actions will shape your future.

The Firefighter's Code for Action

- Stay calm under pressure.
- Stick to the plan.
- Move with purpose.
- Never leave anyone behind—including yourself.
- When in doubt—act with courage.

Act With Purpose, or Drift in Regret

You will either move forward with intention or drift backward with excuses.

You've come too far to stop now. This is your call to action. This is your moment to prove to yourself that you're not just a thinker—you're a doer. You're a fighter. You're a winner.

Real-World Application: From Fireground to Life

Chapter 8 – Act

On the fireground, hesitation can cost lives. Once you've assessed and accepted the situation, taking decisive action is crucial. Whether it's advancing the hose line, performing a search, or rescuing a victim, every second counts. The ability to act confidently, even under pressure, saves lives and prevents the fire from spreading.

In life, taking action after you've made your decision is just as important. Planning and mindset only get you so far—without action, nothing changes. Acting means committing fully to your goals and pushing through fear, doubt, and uncertainty. It means showing up, doing the work, and learning from the results.

Just like in firefighting, your success in life depends on your willingness to move forward, adapt on the fly, and keep pressing ahead even when things get tough.

📝 Chapter 8 Worksheet – Act

1. What is the first action step in your MAP Plan? Have you completed it? If not, when will you?

2. List 3 daily habits that align with your goal.

   _____

   _____

   _____

3. What obstacle has kept you from acting in the past? How will you overcome it now?

   _____

4. Who do you need to ignore in order to stay focused? Who do you need to listen to?

   Ignore: ____

   Listen to: ____

5. What would taking action every day for the next 30 days look like? Describe it.

_____

6. Write a power phrase you will repeat to yourself when you feel hesitation.

_____

_____

📖 Journal Prompt – Act

"Where in my life am I still waiting instead of doing? What would happen if I started today, with what I have, exactly where I am?"

Chapter Nine

Accomplish

Step 5: Accomplish – Get the Job Done

You've made it through the fire. You've assessed your situation honestly. You've accepted your reality without excuses. You've adapted by creating a MAP Plan—Methodical, Ambitious, and Punctual. You've taken bold action. Now comes the step that defines success:

You must accomplish.

There's no glory in starting something that you don't finish. This is the moment where all the work, all the resilience, all the suffering has a payoff. Without accomplishment, the 6 A's to Succeed are just motions. Accomplishment is where the transformation becomes real, where the adversity becomes a steppingstone—not a stopping point.

Completion is Non-Negotiable

To accomplish means to complete the mission—to get the job done. Not half-finished. Not paused. Not one day. Now. If you haven't yet succeeded, that doesn't mean failure. It means feedback. Failure is simply a checkpoint. It's not the end; it's the opportunity to realign and go again.

And if you fail again? Good. That means you're in the fight. You're learning, growing, evolving. Go back to Step 1.

Assess again. Accept again. Adapt again. Act again. And come back here. Come back until it's done.

The Power of Will

In the Firefighter Mindset, skill matters. But will matters more.

"Your will must be stronger than your skill."

It's your will that gets you up after failure. It's your will that pushes you forward when the finish line is still miles away. It's your will that gets the job done when everything inside you screams to quit.

The fire doesn't wait. The job doesn't pause. When you're in the heat of adversity, you don't stop until it's finished. You don't stop until it's done.

That's the mindset of a firefighter. That's the mindset of a winner.

Find Your Why

Your why is your engine. Without a strong reason, your plan will stall. You must dig deep. Find the real reason you're pushing through this adversity. Is it your children? Your purpose? Your peace of mind? Your legacy?

"If your why is big enough, you'll get through any how."

When your why is clear, you become unstoppable.

The Thin Path

Success is a narrow path. It's not glamorous. It's not easy. It's not for the faint-hearted. It's sober. It's focused. It's precise. No self-sabotage. No drinking. No drifting. Just steady, disciplined progress.

Yes, sometimes you'll slip. But you don't quit. You get back on the path.

Gratitude in Adversity

In your darkest moments, be grateful. This isn't just a nice idea—it's a mental weapon. A grateful heart has no room for depression. A grateful mind is calm and focused. Gratitude is the compass that points you back to your strength.

Small Wins, Big Impact

Don't just wait for the big goal to be proud. Celebrate every little step. Paid a bill? Accomplishment. Went to the gym? Accomplishment. Made it through the day without quitting? That's a huge win.

Adversity is overcome one small victory at a time.

Don't Self-Sabotage

One of the biggest reasons people fail to accomplish is that deep down, they don't feel they deserve to succeed. That's a lie. You are worthy. You deserve to finish strong. You have the right to succeed. It's time to get out of your own way.

The Final Push: Finish the Job

You must complete what you started. Even if you feel broken. Even if you're unsure. Even if it's rough around the edges.

You've got to:

- Show up.
- Do the work.
- Stay on mission.
- Get the job done.

Success isn't just about accomplishment. It's about sustaining that accomplishment, continuing the mission every day. Every win must be protected. Every victory maintained.

Real-World Application: From Fireground to Life

Chapter 9 – Accomplish

On the fireground, accomplishing the mission means successfully extinguishing the fire, rescuing those in danger, and securing the scene. It's the moment when all your preparation, decision-making, and actions come together to achieve the goal. The sense of accomplishment fuels your confidence and reinforces the value of your training and teamwork.

In life, accomplishment is about reaching your goals—big or small—and recognizing the effort it took to get there. It's the payoff for persistence, discipline, and resilience. Celebrating your accomplishments keeps you motivated and builds momentum for future challenges. Like a firefighter completing a successful operation, you gain pride and clarity, ready to face the next mission with even greater strength.

Worksheet – Chapter Nine "Accomplish"

1. Define Your Goal
- What is the exact outcome you are working toward?

2. What Does Finishing Look Like?
- Describe the moment you will know the job is done.

3. Identify Obstacles
- What are the possible reasons you might quit?
- How will you counter those?

4. Clarify Your Why
- What's your deepest reason for accomplishing this goal?

5. Mini-Milestones
- What small wins have you had this week?
- What will your next small win be?

6. Eliminate Self-Sabotage
- What habits or thoughts are blocking you?
- Write down one habit to stop this week.

7. Emergency Motivation
- On the days you want to quit, what phrase or quote will you say to yourself?

Journal Prompt – "Accomplish"

"When I look back on this chapter of my life, what will I be proud I finished? What part of me is being strengthened through this fire, and how will I carry that strength forward?"

Write for 10–15 minutes. Be brutally honest. This is your moment.

Chapter Ten

Appreciate

Step 6 of the Firefighter Mindset: APPRECIATE

Once you've Accomplished your mission—whatever your personal battle or professional goal—there is one final, vital step: Appreciate.

Appreciation is not a luxury. It's not optional. It is necessary to lock in your growth, solidify your mindset, and prepare for the next mountain ahead.

Many people race to the finish line only to rush past the moment of victory. They don't pause. They don't reflect. They don't acknowledge what they've been through and how far they've come. Without appreciation, even success can feel hollow. That's not the Firefighter way.

Why Appreciation Matters

The moment you accomplish something significant, you are no longer the person you were when you started. You have evolved. You are stronger, wiser, and more capable. To truly own your growth, you must stop and take stock.

Appreciation helps you:
- Solidify the lessons learned from your journey
- Honour the failures that refined you

- Recognize the people (and perhaps God or the universe) who supported you
- See yourself clearly as the winner you've become
- Build the emotional and spiritual strength to sustain your success

Don't Fall Back

Here's a trap many fall into the moment the problem is fixed or the goal is reached, they relax. They drop their standards. They fall back into old habits. That's how setbacks return.

Appreciation isn't just about gratitude—it's about mindfulness. It's your check-in point. Your reinforcement. Your pivot toward sustainability.

You've climbed a mountain. Now it's time to claim the view—and plan how to keep that summit in sight.

You Have Greatness in You

You must recognize the greatness that got you here. You did this. No matter how small or large your victory seems, you are capable of change, achievement, and perseverance. And if you did it once, you can do it again. And again.

Sustainability begins with appreciation. Celebrate your win. Lock in the lesson. Let the feeling of victory shape your mindset going forward.

The Danger of Forgetting

If you don't appreciate your growth, you'll forget how much it took to get here. And you risk slipping back. Appreciate means remembering your pain and celebrating your strength. It means guarding what you've built and not growing complacent.

The Firefighter Mindset at Completion

When the fire is out, we don't forget the flames. We remember what it took to fight. We remember who we became in the process.

We appreciate the struggle.

We appreciate the transformation.

We appreciate that we didn't quit.

🔥 Real-World Application: From Fireground to Life

Chapter 10 – Appreciate

On the fireground, appreciation is often shown in the form of respect for your team, gratitude for safety, and recognition of the small wins—like successfully rescuing a life or preventing a fire from spreading. Taking a moment to appreciate your fellow firefighters' efforts, the tools at your disposal, and the training that prepared you can boost morale and foster stronger bonds in high-pressure situations.

In life, appreciation means recognizing and valuing the people, opportunities, and experiences that support your growth. It's about cultivating gratitude even when things are tough, which builds resilience and a positive mindset. By appreciating what you have, you create a foundation of mental strength and contentment that empowers you to keep pushing forward in your personal and professional life.

Worksheets: Chapter Ten – Appreciate

🔸 Worksheet 1: Recognizing the Win

1. What have you recently accomplished?

   Be specific. Name the goal or adversity you overcame.

2. What qualities in yourself helped you accomplish it?

   e.g., discipline, resilience, humility, patience, courage.

3. What challenges did you overcome along the way?

   Reflect on setbacks and how you handled them.

4. Who helped or supported you on your journey?

   List names, resources, even books or beliefs that guided you.

5. What emotions are you feeling now that you've reached this stage?

   Describe honestly: relief, joy, pride, peace, fatigue?

🔸 Worksheet 2: Locking in Your Growth

1. In what ways have you changed during this journey?

   Mentally, emotionally, spiritually, physically?

2. What do you understand now that you didn't before?

3. What habits helped you get here?

Which ones should you continue?

4. What old habits or patterns must you leave behind?

5. How can you remind yourself of your growth regularly?

Create rituals, affirmations, or visual cues.

🔥 Worksheet 3: Sustainability & Prevention

1. What does "sustaining this win" look like in your daily life?

2. What systems or support will help you maintain your success?

3. What are your red flags—signs you're slipping back?

4. How will you respond if those red flags show up?

5. What's the next mission or area in your life that now needs your Firefighter Mindset?

Journal Prompts: Chapter Ten – Appreciate

1. "I am proud of myself because…"

(Write a full page of reasons.)

2. "To honour my journey, I will…"

(Describe how you will celebrate, remember, and sustain your progress.)

3. "I appreciate the following people and experiences for shaping my growth…"

(Be generous with your gratitude.)

4. "I used to be the kind of person who ____, but now I ____."

(Recognize your transformation.)

5. "My greatest lesson from this accomplishment is…"

(Seal it with reflection.)

Chapter Eleven

Firefighter Fitness

The Discipline of Daily Strength

The Firefighter Fitness Code

Let me be real with you — I'm not a doctor, dietician, or Instagram fitness influencer. But what I am is living proof that you can change your life with consistency, self-respect, and the Firefighter Mindset. I've been in the game for decades — featured in firefighter calendars, working as a glamour model, and still keeping my health sharp into my 50s. But I didn't start there. I was an obese kid, hiding behind food and fighting shame. I know the pain of feeling judged in a swimming pool changing room or on a rugby pitch.

What changed? I did.

What saved me? Discipline, consistency, training — and food.

This isn't about fads. It's not a 30-day shred or some supplement scheme. It's about making physical wellbeing a way of life — your firefighter fitness protocol.

Fitness: Structure Over Speed

Cardio:

- Start slow. Brisk walking or light jogging — 30 mins daily minimum, 3–7 days per week.
- Goal: Work up to 60 minutes. No need to sprint. Firefighters move efficiently, not recklessly.

Strength training:

- Body Split:
  o Chest & biceps
  o Shoulders & triceps
  o Back & legs
  o Core daily (sit-ups, planks)
- Timeframe: 20–40 mins per session
- Tools: Light weights, resistance bands, bodyweight
- Daily sit-ups: Start with 3 sets of 10, build up to 3 sets of 40.

Swimming:

- As often as possible – tones skin, targets facial fat, and slims the chin line.

Stomach toning:

- Abdominal belts: Use consistently (morning & night, even while driving)

Golden Rule:

No steroids. No slimming pills. No protein shakes. No cheat codes.

Just discipline, commitment, and honest work.

Nutrition: What Fuels the Firefighter Mindset

🔥 Best Sources of Protein

• Meats: Chicken breast, turkey, lean beef, lamb, steak, ham, gammon

• Fish: Tuna, salmon, sardines, mackerel

• Dairy: Eggs, Greek yogurt, cottage cheese, hard cheese

• Other: Liver, bacon (minimal processing), milk (whole or semi-skimmed)

🍚 Best Sources of Carbohydrates (Complex + Nutrient-Dense)

• Grains: Quinoa, oats, brown rice, barley

• Vegetables: Sweet potatoes, broccoli, spinach, kale

• Legumes: Lentils, chickpeas, black beans

• Fruits: Berries, apples, oranges (in moderation)

Avoid: White bread, fried chips, sugary cereals, pastries, and fruit juices.

🥑 Best Sources of Healthy Fats

• Oils: Olive oil, avocado oil, flaxseed oil

• Nuts & Seeds: Almonds, walnuts, chia seeds, flaxseeds

• Others: Avocados, fatty fish (like salmon), natural peanut butter (no added sugar)

💧 Water Intake: Daily Recommendations

- Men: 3.7 litres (about 15.5 cups)
- Women: 2.7 litres (about 11.5 cups)
- Children (age 4–13): 1.3–2.1 litres (based on age/gender)
- Drink more if you exercise, live in a hot climate, or are ill.

Skip fizzy drinks, alcohol, and sugar-loaded juices. Use sparkling water or flavoured teas instead if needed.

The Mindset Behind the Muscle

Firefighter Fitness isn't about six-packs or Instagram likes. It's about readiness — physical, mental, and emotional. It's about building the body and discipline that can withstand adversity. The gym taught me confidence, not just how to fight. The London Fire Brigade taught me pressure. And life taught me how to handle both.

Bullies couldn't stop me. Critics couldn't break me. Excuses never got a look-in.

The question is: what's stopping you?

Real-World Application: From Fireground to Life

Chapter 11 – Firefighter Fitness

On the fireground, physical fitness isn't just a bonus—it's a necessity. Your stamina, strength, and agility directly affect your ability to perform lifesaving tasks under extreme conditions. Being fit reduces the risk of injury, helps you endure long, exhausting shifts, and allows you to react quickly and effectively when every second counts.

In life, maintaining fitness translates to better overall health, increased energy, and mental clarity. It builds discipline and confidence that spill over into your daily routines and challenges. Prioritizing your fitness is an investment in your longevity and ability to handle whatever life throws your way—both on and off the fireground.

Firefighter Fitness Worksheet

1. My Fitness Why:

Why do I want to be fitter and stronger?

→

2. My Weekly Plan (Initial):

- Days I will train this week:

→

- Cardio:

→

- Strength focus:

→

- Recovery plan (stretching, rest, etc.):

→

3. Nutrition Non-Negotiables:

- Three foods I will remove from my diet immediately:

→

- Three healthy alternatives I will commit to:

→

4. Weekly Water Check:

- Litres per day goal:

→

- How I'll track it:

→

🧠 Journal Prompts: Fire in the Mind

1. What's one time in my life when I felt strong, capable, and in control of my body? What made it possible?

→

2. What beliefs or past experiences have made me doubt my ability to be fit or healthy? How do I rewrite that story now?

→

3. What does a 'fit version' of me feel like, act like, think like? How does this version handle stress or temptation?

→

4. How has physical pain, discomfort, or shame impacted my confidence? How can movement now become a source of power?

→

5. What does it mean to me to have the Firefighter Mindset — physically, mentally, spiritually?

→

Final Words

Fitness is not about being shredded — it's about being ready.

Ready to carry someone. Ready to run through hell. Ready to carry yourself when no one else will.

You don't need steroids. You need standards.

You don't need a fast fix. You need a forever focus.

You don't need more motivation. You need a mission.

That's the Firefighter Mindset.

Chapter Twelve

The Conclusion

The Firefighter Mindset: No Surrender, No Retreat

The Firefighter Mindset is more than just a strategy—it's a survival system. A blueprint forged in flames, pressure, sweat, and soul. I didn't read it in a textbook. I lived it through fire calls, tragedy, loss, and my own personal hells. It's not endorsed by the London Fire Brigade—it's endorsed by scars, second chances, and the stubborn refusal to quit.

This mindset kept me going through fires that threatened lives—and through emotional infernos that threatened mine. It isn't perfect. It's not pretty. But it gets the job done.

I didn't write this book to become some self-help guru or motivational poser. I wrote it because if it helps just one person get back on their feet, then every page has been worth it.

Whether you're trying to lose weight, get back up after heartbreak, rebuild your confidence, or chase that dream everyone told you to forget—this book is your siren call. Your reminder that you are not done. That you've got more fight left in you.

The Power of the Firefighter Mindset

What makes it powerful? It was built to save lives—literally. In firefighting, failure isn't an option. You can't afford to panic. You can't wait for someone else. You assess, adapt, and act. Then you finish the job.

The Firefighter Mindset is built on robustness, resilience, and reality.

It's self-reliant because sometimes all you've got is yourself.

It's adaptable because no two fires—or life challenges—are the same.

And it's honest because sugar-coating doesn't stop flames.

The same system that helped me navigate burning buildings helped me rebuild my body, mind, and life.

The System Recap – From Firefighting to Life-Fighting

1. Make the Decision.

Decide you are not going down. This is your comeback moment, not your collapse.

2. Embrace the S.E.A. of Change.

    Start – Begin now. Even if it's messy.

    Endure – Stay in it when it's hard.

    Accomplish – Finish. No hesitating at the finish line.

3. Discover Your Why.

Make it personal. Make it powerful. Your 'why' will get you out of bed when motivation dies.

4. Use the 6 A's to Succeed.

>   Assess
>
>   Accept
>
>   Adapt
>
>   Act
>
>   Accomplish
>
>   Appreciate

5. The M.A.P Plan.

A no-nonsense action plan to get moving:

>   Motivation
>
>   Action
>
>   Discipline

6. Appreciate the Wins (and the Losses).

Don't just move on. Reflect. Appreciate your journey. Don't come out bitter—come out better. Wisdom over wounds.

Remember:

- ✸ You are more powerful than your pain.
- ✸ You are stronger than your situation.
- ✸ You are one decision away from changing your life.

🔥 Real-World Application: From Fireground to Life

Chapter 12 – The Conclusion

On the fireground, every call ends with reflection—what went right, what could be improved, and how to grow stronger for the next mission. The conclusion isn't just the end; it's the preparation for what's next. It's about learning from every experience and committing to continuous improvement.

In life, the conclusion of your journey isn't a final stop—it's a new beginning. Embracing this mindset means recognizing that growth never ends. Whether you've faced setbacks or triumphs, you use those lessons to build a better version of yourself. Like a firefighter who never stops training, you keep moving forward, stronger, wiser, and ready for whatever comes next.

Final thoughts

Always remember you are already enough. You already have within you the power to cope and deal with everything and to overcome anything. Remember, just do it, don't think and take one step after another. Keep going, never retreat, never surrender. It is amazing what a human being can do, if they must. You have greatness already within.

Your perception and intent will manifest your life.

Control your perception and intent and you manifest whatever life you truly want.

Be tough!

Toughness combined with compassion creates character in a person. Character combined with competence creates in a person, a conqueror!

A conqueror controls their destiny!

'Tough people create opportunities for everyone to shine, weak people create opportunities for everyone to suffer.'

'Viruses' and 'Medicines'

There are two types of people in this world, in your private life and at work. The two types are 'viruses' and 'medicines'

A person that is a virus, is that type of person that no matter where they are, will always deteriorate the situation and disrupt and destroy things whether it's a personal relationship or a work environment.

A virus person will come in and contaminate everything around them, in a negative way. They will always criticise and be negative. They will always just seek to drain and use a person. It is VERY important to stay away from viruses, stay away from those people for they will contaminate your life, deteriorate it and destroy anything healthy about it.

Alternatively, there is another type of person in life. These people are the medicines. These are types of people that will come into your life and improve it and even solve issues. These people will come into your life and instantly make things seem better. Like a cure to your life's adversities, they will influence things in a constructive way. Being supportive and positive, these types of people don't moan or criticise. If they haven't got a good word to say about someone, they won't say anything at all.

Medicine people are the opposite to virus people and like medicine they will help support and even solve problems in your life. It is VERY important to surround yourself with this type of people. Surround yourself with the medicines in life and avoid the viruses. There will be some people who will have varying levels of being medicines or being viruses. Seek out the medicines in life not the viruses, cut out any viruses in your life. Additionally, ask yourself what type of person are you? are you a virus or a medicine in life? Always strive to be more like a medicine to yourself and other people around you. Remember, nobody wants a virus in their life and the medicines in life will always be welcome.

Faith

Finally, the antidote to fear is faith. Always have faith in yourself and God.

Worksheet – Lock In the Mindset

Question

Your Answer

What adversity are you facing right now?

Have you fully accepted this is your reality? (Be honest)

What's your first action step, today?

What's your "Why"? (Deep and personal)

What does success look like in this situation?

What does "accomplishment" mean to you?

How will you appreciate your progress, no matter how small?

Journal Prompts

1. When in your life have you shown the Firefighter Mindset before? Describe it.

2. What have you endured that most people would have quit on?

3. How can your pain be turned into power?

4. What does "never surrender, never retreat" mean to you personally?

5. What will your life look like after you accomplish your next big goal?

Quote to End With:

"You don't need a cape to be a hero. Just guts, grit, and the refusal to quit." — Firefighter Mindset

Remembering the 343 firefighters who gave their lives at the World Trade Center in New York City on 11th Sept 2001

and

all the firefighters who have made the ultimate sacrifice to save others.

'Never Retreat, Never Surrender'

Coming soon

'The Father Figure'
Forbidden Fatherly Wisdom